EXPLORE CANADA

Travel Guide to National Parks for Outdoor Adventurers

The Citi-scaper

Copyright © 2023 by The Citi-scaper

This guidebook is the original and exclusive property of Citi-scaper, protected by international copyright laws. Reproduction, distribution, or transmission of this material in any form, electronic or mechanical, is strictly prohibited without prior written consent from The Citi-scaper.

The contents of this guide are a result of extensive research and field testing conducted by The Citi-scaper's team of expert travel writers. We intend to provide practical and useful information to travelers, with accuracy and currency at the time of publication. However, we do not make any guarantees, express or implied, regarding the completeness or accuracy of the information provided.

The Citi-scaper reserves the right to update and revise the content of this guide without prior notice. We appreciate your respect for the intellectual property of our team at The Citi-scaper and wish you happy travels.

Table of Contents

EXPLORE CANADA   1
Introduction   7
Chapter 1   11
Overview   11
   History   13
   Why Visit?   16
   When to Visit   18
   Significance of National Parks   19
Chapter 2   25
Planning Your Trip   25
   How to Get There   26
   Where to Stay   27
   What to Pack   28
   Safety Tips   29
Chapter 3   31
Banff National Park   31
   Overview   31
   History and Geography   32
   Getting There and Around   32
   Popular Activities and Attractions   33
   Travel Tips   35
Chapter 4   39
Jasper National Park   39
   Overview   39
   History and Geography   40

Getting There and Around	40
Activities	41
Travel Tips	45
Chapter 5	**49**
Yoho National Park	**49**
Overview	49
History and Geography	49
Getting There and Around	50
Popular Activities and Attractions	51
Travel Tips	54
Chapter 6	**57**
Kootenay National Park	**57**
Overview	57
History and Geography	58
Getting There and Around	58
Popular Activities and Attractions	60
Travel Tips	62
Chapter 7	**65**
Glacier National Park	**65**
Overview	65
History and Geography	66
Getting There and Around	66
Popular Activities	68
Attractions	70
Travel Tips	72
Chapter 8	**75**
Waterton Lakes National Park	**75**

Overview	75
History and Geography	76
Getting There and Around	77
Popular Activities	79
Attractions	81
Travel Tips	83
Chapter 9	**85**
Wood Buffalo National Park	**85**
Overview	85
History and Geography	86
Getting There and Around	87
Popular Activities	88
Attractions	90
Travel Tips	92
Chapter 10	**95**
Prince Albert National Park	**95**
Overview	95
History and Geography	96
Getting There and Around	96
Popular Activities	98
Attractions	100
Travel Tips	102
Chapter 11	**105**
Fundy National Park	**105**
Overview	105
History and Geography	106
Getting There and Around	107

Popular Activities	108
Attractions	109
Travel Tips	110
Chapter 12	**113**
Cape Breton Highlands National Park	**113**
Overview	113
History and Geography	114
Getting There and Around	114
Popular Attractions	116
Activities	118
Travel Tips	120
Chapter 13	**123**
Activities in the National Parks	**123**
Hiking	123
Wildlife Viewing	124
Camping	124
Canoeing and Kayaking	125
Winter Sports	125
Chapter 14	**127**
Beyond the National Parks	**127**
Other Natural Attractions	127
Cities and Towns Worth Visiting	128
Cultural and Historical Sites	129
Permits, Fees, and Regulations	131
Dining Options	133
Conclusion	**135**
TRAVEL PLANNERS	**137**

Introduction

Canada is a country that is synonymous with natural beauty. From the towering peaks of the Rocky Mountains to the rugged coastline of the Atlantic provinces, this vast country is home to some of the most stunning landscapes on the planet. And perhaps nowhere is this more evident than in Canada's national parks.

In this guidebook, we invite you to explore Canada's natural wonders through its national parks. We've compiled all the information you need to plan a memorable trip, whether you're a seasoned outdoor enthusiast or a first-time visitor. From hiking trails to wildlife viewing opportunities, we'll take you on a journey through some of Canada's most spectacular natural landscapes.

Our guidebook is organized into several sections. In the first section, we'll introduce you to the national park system in Canada, including a brief history and the importance of conservation efforts. Then, we'll dive into the practical details of planning your trip, including when to go, how to get there, and where to stay.

In the heart of the guidebook, you'll find detailed descriptions of some of Canada's most popular national parks, including Banff, Jasper, Yoho, Waterton Lakes, and Kootenay. We'll provide an overview of each park's unique features, the best activities to do, and the most popular hiking trails. We'll also give you insider tips on where to spot wildlife, the best places to camp, and nearby attractions worth checking out.

But the national parks aren't just about hiking and camping. In the fourth section, we'll explore other activities you can do in the parks, such as fishing, wildlife viewing, and winter sports. We'll also give you tips on scenic drives and other natural attractions you won't want to miss.

Finally, in the last section of the guidebook, we'll take you beyond the national parks and explore other natural attractions, cities, and towns worth visiting, as well as cultural and historical sites.

Whether you're planning your first trip to Canada's national parks or you're a seasoned adventurer looking to explore more of this beautiful country, our guidebook has something for everyone. So grab your hiking boots, pack your bags, and get ready to explore Canada's natural wonders like never before.

Chapter 1

Overview

Canada is home to numerous natural wonders, including breathtaking landscapes, diverse wildlife, and unique ecosystems. These wonders are protected and preserved within the country's 48 national parks, which collectively span over 300,000 square kilometers.

Some of the most famous natural wonders within Canada's national parks include the Canadian Rocky Mountains, which are home to Banff National Park and Jasper National Park. These parks offer stunning vistas of towering peaks, pristine lakes, and cascading waterfalls. Visitors can also enjoy hiking, skiing, and wildlife viewing in the area.

Another popular natural wonder is the Nahanni National Park Reserve, which features the South Nahanni River, one of the world's most dramatic whitewater rivers, and the Virginia Falls, which are twice the height of Niagara Falls.

In addition to these natural wonders, Canada's national parks are home to a variety of ecosystems, from the coastal rainforests of Pacific Rim National Park Reserve to the tundra and polar regions of Auyuittuq National Park.

The parks are also home to a vast array of wildlife, including grizzly bears, wolves, moose, caribou, and polar bears, to name just a few. Visitors can observe these animals in their natural habitats through guided tours or self-guided hikes.

Overall, Canada's national parks offer a unique opportunity to experience the country's natural beauty and biodiversity, making them a must-see destination for nature lovers and outdoor enthusiasts.

History

The idea of setting aside land for public use and enjoyment is not a new one. In fact, the first national park in the world, Yellowstone National Park, was established in the United States in 1872. Canada followed suit in 1885 with the creation of Banff National Park, which is often referred to as the birthplace of Canada's national parks system.

Banff National Park was initially established to protect the hot springs that had become a popular tourist attraction. The federal government of Canada recognized the need to protect this unique natural wonder, and so it set aside a large area of land around the hot springs. This was the first step in what would become a long and storied history of national park creation in Canada.

Over the next few decades, more national parks were established across the country. Jasper National Park was created in 1907, followed by Yoho National Park in 1909. These parks were established to protect the natural beauty of the Rocky Mountains, which were becoming increasingly popular with tourists and explorers.

In the 1920s and 1930s, the national parks system in Canada underwent significant changes. The federal government established the Dominion Parks Branch, which was responsible for managing the national parks. The Branch also began to take a more active role in promoting tourism and encouraging visitors to explore the parks.

During this time, several iconic structures were built in the national parks, including the Banff Springs Hotel and the Chateau Lake Louise. These grand hotels were designed to attract wealthy tourists and provide them with a luxurious base from which to explore the parks.

In the years following World War II, the national parks system in Canada continued to grow. New parks were established in every region of the country, from the rugged coastline of Pacific Rim National Park Reserve to the remote wilderness of Auyuittuq National Park.

Today, Canada's national parks are visited by millions of people each year. They are a testament to the country's commitment to preserving its natural heritage for future generations. Visitors can explore pristine forests, rugged mountains, and stunning coastlines, all while learning about the history of these remarkable places.

Canada's national parks are some of the most iconic and beautiful natural areas in the world. Understanding the history of these parks can help visitors to appreciate the natural beauty of these places even more. From the establishment of Banff National Park in 1885 to the creation of new parks in every region of the country, Canada's national parks have a rich and fascinating history that is just waiting to be explored.

Why Visit?

Canada is a country blessed with awe-inspiring natural beauty, from rugged coastlines and towering mountains to lush forests and pristine lakes. The national parks in Canada are some of the most breathtaking natural wonders in the world, attracting millions of people yearly. If you're an outdoor adventurer, then Canada's national parks should be on your bucket list, and this chapter will give you a glimpse of why.

One of the primary reasons to visit Canada's national parks is their incredible natural beauty. Each park has its unique features, from the turquoise waters of Banff's Moraine Lake to the massive glaciers of Jasper's Columbia Icefield. The beauty of Canada's national parks is so mesmerizing that they have been featured in numerous movies, TV shows, and commercials.

Beyond their beauty, Canada's national parks offer a wide range of outdoor activities, making them ideal for outdoor enthusiasts. For example, Banff National Park is famous for its extensive network of hiking trails, including the popular Plain of Six Glaciers Trail, while Jasper National Park offers fantastic opportunities for wildlife viewing, with elk, moose, bighorn sheep, and black bears all regularly spotted in the park.

In addition to outdoor activities, Canada's national parks are also a great place to learn about the country's history and culture. Many parks have significant cultural and historical sites that tell the stories of the people who have lived in the area for thousands of years. For example, in Gros Morne National Park in Newfoundland, you can learn about the geology of the park and its cultural history through guided hikes and interpretive programs.

Moreover, visiting Canada's national parks is an excellent way to disconnect from the busyness of daily life and immerse yourself in nature. Whether you're camping in the backcountry or enjoying a leisurely stroll along a scenic trail, the parks offer a chance to slow down and appreciate the natural world around you. In the words of the renowned conservationist John Muir, "Nature's peace will flow into you as sunshine flows into trees."

Finally, Canada's national parks are a testament to the country's commitment to conservation and environmental protection. The parks are home to diverse ecosystems, and their preservation is critical for the survival of countless plant and animal species. By visiting the parks, you are not only experiencing their natural beauty but also supporting their conservation efforts.

Canada's national parks are a treasure trove of natural wonders, outdoor activities, cultural and historical significance, and environmental conservation efforts. They are a must-visit destination for any outdoor adventurer looking to experience the beauty and majesty of the Canadian wilderness.

When to Visit

The best time to visit Canada's National Parks depends on the region and the activities you want to do. The summer months, from June to September, are the most popular and busy times to visit, with long days and mild weather. However, this also means more crowds and higher prices. If you prefer quieter and less expensive times to visit, consider the shoulder seasons in the spring and fall.

For example, if you want to visit Banff National Park to avoid the crowds, consider visiting in September. The weather is still pleasant, and the foliage is starting to change colors, making for a beautiful and peaceful experience. Additionally, if you want to go skiing or snowshoeing in Jasper National Park, the best time to visit is from December to February when there is plenty of snow on the ground.

Significance of National Parks

National parks in Canada are not only significant but also essential for several reasons. These parks are not just a source of natural beauty and outdoor recreation but also play a vital role in protecting and preserving the country's natural heritage and biodiversity.

Firstly, national parks in Canada are critical for the conservation of biodiversity. Canada has a diverse range of flora and fauna, with many species found nowhere else in the world. These parks are designed to protect the natural ecosystems that support the country's unique and often fragile plant and animal species. By preserving these ecosystems, national parks help to maintain the natural balance of ecosystems and ensure the long-term survival of many species.

Secondly, national parks in Canada provide a range of recreational opportunities for visitors, which have significant economic benefits. Millions of people visit Canada's national parks each year, and the tourism industry generated by these parks creates jobs, boosts local economies, and provides opportunities for small businesses. Moreover, these parks provide Canadians with affordable and accessible recreational opportunities, promoting healthy lifestyles and wellbeing.

Thirdly, national parks in Canada serve as outdoor classrooms, where people can learn about natural history, ecology, and conservation. Many of these parks have interpretive centers, guided hikes, and educational programs that provide visitors with an opportunity to learn about the natural world, cultural heritage, and conservation issues. This educational aspect of national parks is particularly crucial in fostering environmental awareness and inspiring people to take action to protect the natural world.

Fourthly, national parks in Canada serve as important sites of cultural and historical significance. These parks preserve and celebrate the rich cultural heritage of indigenous peoples, early settlers, and other groups that have shaped Canada's history. They also provide an opportunity for people to reconnect with nature and their cultural roots, promoting cultural diversity and understanding.

Finally, national parks in Canada serve as a testament to the country's commitment to conservation and environmental protection. These parks are managed according to strict conservation principles, ensuring that they remain ecologically sustainable and resilient in the face of threats such as climate change, habitat fragmentation, and invasive species.

In conclusion, national parks in Canada are significant for a range of reasons, including biodiversity conservation, economic benefits, education, cultural and historical significance, and environmental protection. These parks are an essential part of Canada's natural heritage and serve as an example of the country's commitment to preserving and protecting its natural resources for future generations.

Benefits of Visiting National Parks

Visiting national parks can provide numerous benefits for individuals, families, and communities. National parks offer a wide range of recreational activities, educational opportunities, and a chance to connect with nature. Here are some of the benefits of visiting national parks:

Health Benefits: Visiting national parks and spending time in nature has been linked to a range of health benefits. Research has shown that spending time in nature can help reduce stress, lower blood pressure, boost the immune system, and improve overall mental and physical health.

Educational Opportunities: National parks offer visitors an opportunity to learn about natural history, ecology, and conservation. Parks often have interpretive centers, guided hikes, and educational programs that provide visitors with a chance to learn about the natural world and the importance of conservation.

Outdoor Recreation: National parks offer a wide range of outdoor activities, including hiking, camping, fishing, boating, skiing, and wildlife viewing. These activities provide visitors with an opportunity to connect with nature, get exercise, and enjoy the outdoors.

Cultural and Historical Significance: Many national parks have significant cultural and historical sites that tell the stories of the people who have lived in the area for thousands of years. These sites provide an opportunity for visitors to learn about the history and culture of the region and gain a deeper appreciation of its significance.

Environmental Conservation: National parks play a crucial role in preserving and protecting natural ecosystems and biodiversity. By visiting national parks, visitors support conservation efforts and help to maintain the natural balance of ecosystems, ensuring the long-term survival of many plant and animal species.

Economic Benefits: National parks also provide significant economic benefits, supporting local communities and small businesses. The tourism industry generated by national parks creates jobs, boosts local economies, and provides opportunities for small businesses.

Visiting national parks can provide a range of benefits, including improved health, educational opportunities, outdoor recreation, cultural and historical significance, environmental conservation, and economic benefits. These parks are essential resources for individuals, families, and communities, offering a chance to connect with nature and gain a deeper appreciation of our natural heritage.

Chapter 2

Planning Your Trip

Exploring Canada's natural wonders is an experience of a lifetime, and to make the most out of your trip, careful planning is essential. When planning your trip, consider your budget, interests, and travel companions. Canada's National Parks are spread throughout the country and offer a variety of outdoor activities, from hiking to camping and wildlife viewing.

One crucial aspect of planning your trip is determining the best time to visit. Each National Park has its own unique charm, and the best time to visit varies depending on what you want to see and do. For example, if you want to see the Northern Lights, plan your visit to Jasper National Park between November and March. However, if you're interested in wildlife viewing, you may want to visit Banff National Park in the summer when animals are more active.

Another essential aspect of planning your trip is determining how much time you have available. Canada's National Parks offer a variety of experiences, from short day hikes to multi-day backpacking trips. Determine what activities you want to participate in and allocate enough time to enjoy them fully.

How to Get There

Canada's National Parks are spread across the country, and getting there depends on your starting point and destination. The easiest way to get to most National Parks is by car, as many are located in remote areas without public transportation. If you're traveling from a major city, you can rent a car or take a bus to the nearest town and then rent a car from there.

If you're traveling from Toronto to Algonquin Provincial Park, you can rent a car in Toronto and drive for approximately three hours to the park's entrance. If you're traveling from Vancouver to Banff National Park, you can take a bus or a train to Calgary and then rent a car or take a shuttle to the park.

Where to Stay

Canada's National Parks offer a variety of accommodation options, from camping to hotels and lodges. When choosing where to stay, consider your budget, interests, and travel companions.

Camping is an excellent option for those who want to immerse themselves in nature and save money. Most National Parks have campgrounds with basic amenities, such as picnic tables, fire pits, and washrooms. However, if you're not comfortable camping or prefer more comfortable accommodations, there are plenty of other options, including lodges, cabins, and hotels.

If you're visiting Jasper National Park and want a luxurious experience, consider staying at the Fairmont Jasper Park Lodge. This hotel offers stunning views of the surrounding mountains, a world-class spa, and multiple restaurants. Alternatively, if you're visiting Banff National Park and want a rustic experience, consider staying at one of the park's backcountry lodges, accessible only by hiking or skiing.

What to Pack

When packing for your trip to Canada's National Parks, consider the season, climate, and activities you plan to participate in. Regardless of the season, it's essential to dress in layers and bring warm clothing, as temperatures can drop quickly, especially at higher elevations. If you're planning to hike, bring sturdy and comfortable hiking boots, a backpack, and plenty of water and snacks. Additionally, don't forget to pack sunscreen, insect repellent, and a first-aid kit.

If you're visiting Gros Morne National Park in Newfoundland during the summer, you'll want to bring lightweight clothing, as temperatures can be warm and humid. However, if you plan to hike the Long Range Mountains, bring warm layers, as the weather can be unpredictable and change quickly.

Safety Tips

Exploring Canada's National Parks is a thrilling experience, but it's essential to prioritize safety. Always follow park rules and regulations and respect wildlife and the environment. Additionally, be aware of your surroundings and avoid risky behavior.

When hiking or camping, it's crucial to be prepared and bring essential gear, such as a map, compass, and flashlight. Always let someone know your itinerary and expected return time, and never hike alone.

If you encounter wildlife, give them plenty of space and never approach or feed them. It's also essential to properly store food and garbage to avoid attracting animals to your campsite.

For example, if you're camping in Banff National Park and encounter a bear, slowly back away and speak in a calm voice to avoid startling the animal. Make noise and use bear spray if necessary, and never run away or play dead.

Planning a trip to Canada's National Parks requires careful consideration of several factors, including when to go, how to get there, where to stay, what to pack, and safety tips. With proper planning and preparation, you can have a safe and enjoyable experience exploring Canada's natural wonders.

Chapter 3

Banff National Park

Overview

Banff National Park is a UNESCO World Heritage Site located in Alberta, Canada. It was established in 1885, making it Canada's first national park and one of the world's oldest. The park spans 6,641 square kilometers (2,564 square miles) and is home to a diverse range of landscapes, from towering mountains to alpine meadows, glaciers, and turquoise lakes.

History and Geography

Banff National Park was established after railway workers discovered natural hot springs in the area. The park was originally named "Hot Springs Reserve" and later changed to Banff National Park. The park is located in the Rocky Mountains and includes part of the Great Divide, which separates the rivers that flow to the Pacific Ocean and the Atlantic Ocean. It is also home to the Columbia Icefield, one of the largest ice fields in the Rocky Mountains.

Getting There and Around

Banff National Park is easily accessible by car, bus, or plane. The closest airport is Calgary International Airport, which is about an hour and a half drive from the park. Once in the park, there are several options for getting around, including driving, hiking, biking, and taking public transportation. The park has a shuttle bus service called Roam Transit, which runs throughout the park and is an environmentally friendly option.

Where to stay:

There are several accommodation options in Banff National Park, ranging from camping and RV sites to hotels and lodges. Some popular options include the Fairmont Banff Springs Hotel, the Banff Centre for Arts and Creativity, and the Tunnel Mountain Resort.

Popular Activities and Attractions

Banff National Park offers a wide range of activities and attractions for visitors. Some popular options include:

Soaking in the natural hot springs at the Upper Hot Springs

Taking a scenic drive on the Icefields Parkway

Visiting the Columbia Icefield and walking on the Athabasca Glacier

Hiking to the top of Sulphur Mountain for panoramic views of the park

Going on a wildlife tour to see bears, elk, and other animals

Canoeing or kayaking on one of the park's many lakes

Best hikes and trails:

Banff National Park is known for its incredible hiking trails, ranging from easy walks to challenging hikes. Some popular options include:

Johnston Canyon Trail: a 5.2-kilometer (3.2-mile) round trip hike to a series of waterfalls

Plain of Six Glaciers Trail: a 14-kilometer (8.7-mile) round trip hike with stunning views of glaciers and mountain peaks

Larch Valley Trail: a 4.4-kilometer (2.7-mile) round trip hike with stunning fall colors in September

Sunshine Meadows Trail: a 9.7-kilometer (6-mile) loop trail with panoramic views of the Canadian Rockies

Wildlife and nature watching:

Banff National Park is home to a diverse range of wildlife, including grizzly bears, black bears, moose, elk, and bighorn sheep. Visitors should always keep a safe distance from wildlife and follow the park's guidelines for wildlife viewing. The park also has several areas for bird watching, including the Cave and Basin Marsh.

Travel Tips

Plan ahead and make reservations for accommodations and activities in advance

Be prepared for changing weather conditions and bring appropriate gear for hiking and outdoor activities

Follow the park's guidelines for wildlife viewing and always keep a safe distance

Practice Leave No Trace principles and pack out all trash

Respect the park's natural environment and wildlife, and help preserve it for future generations.

Avoid overcrowding popular attractions and consider visiting lesser-known areas of the park

Be aware of park regulations, including trail closures and fire bans

Consider taking a guided tour or hiring a local guide for a more immersive experience and to learn more about the park's history and ecology

Take the time to appreciate the park's natural beauty and connect with nature

Finally, make sure to bring a camera and capture the stunning landscapes and wildlife for lasting memories.

In addition to the above tips, it's important to note that Banff National Park is a popular tourist destination, especially during peak season in the summer months. To avoid crowds, consider visiting during the shoulder season in the spring or fall.

Another important consideration when visiting Banff National Park is the park's ecological fragility. The park's ecosystems are delicate and easily disrupted by human activity. It's important to minimize your impact on the environment by staying on designated trails, not disturbing wildlife or their habitat, and practicing responsible waste management.

If you're planning to go hiking or participate in other outdoor activities, make sure to check the weather and trail conditions before heading out. The park's weather can be unpredictable, and trail conditions can change quickly. Make sure to bring appropriate gear, including layers, a hat, sunscreen, and plenty of water.

Overall, Banff National Park is a breathtaking destination that offers a unique opportunity to connect with nature and explore some of Canada's most stunning natural wonders.

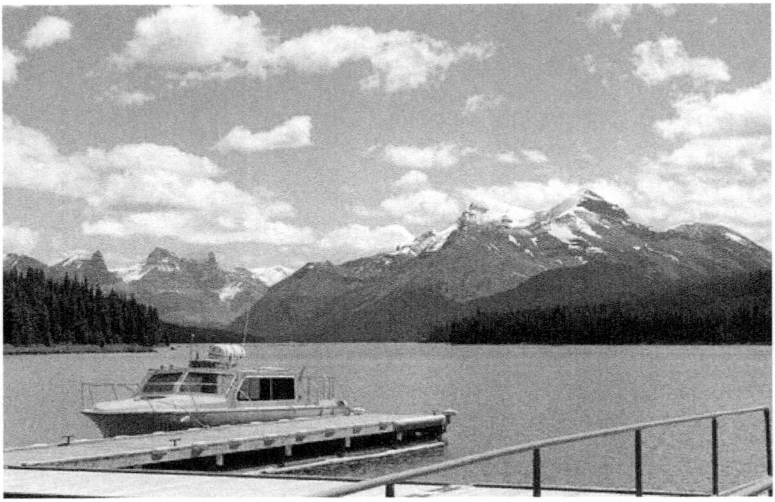

Chapter 4

Jasper National Park

Overview

Jasper National Park is a popular national park in Canada, located in the province of Alberta. It is a natural wonderland that spans over 10,878 square kilometers and is home to some of the most stunning landscapes in the country. The park is situated in the Canadian Rockies and is part of the larger UNESCO World Heritage Site, which includes several other national parks in the area. Jasper National Park is known for its awe-inspiring mountains, glaciers, lakes, rivers, and wildlife, which make it a popular destination for outdoor enthusiasts.

History and Geography

The Park was established in 1907 as a result of the Canadian government's efforts to conserve the natural resources of the area. The park was named after Jasper Hawes, who was a fur trader in the 1800s. The park's landscape is shaped by the Rocky Mountains, which dominate the area, and it is home to several glaciers, including the Columbia Icefield, which is one of the largest ice fields in the world. The park is also home to several lakes, including Maligne Lake, which is the second-largest glacier-fed lake in the world.

Getting There and Around

Jasper National Park is easily accessible by car, with several highways leading to the park, including the Trans-Canada Highway and the Icefields Parkway. The closest major airport is Edmonton International Airport, which is about 4 hours away by car. Once inside the park, visitors can get around by car, bike, or foot.

Where to Stay:

There are several accommodation options within Jasper National Park, ranging from campsites to luxury hotels. Some of the popular options include the Fairmont Jasper Park Lodge, which is a luxurious hotel situated on the shores of Lac Beauvert, and Whistler's Campground, which is a popular spot for campers.

Activities

Visitors to Jasper National Park can enjoy a wide range of outdoor activities, such as hiking, camping, skiing, and wildlife viewing. Some of the most popular activities and attractions in Jasper National Park are:

Maligne Lake: This stunning lake is the largest natural lake in the Canadian Rockies and is a must-see attraction in Jasper National Park. Visitors can take a boat tour or rent a canoe or kayak to explore the lake and its surrounding mountains and glaciers.

Columbia Icefield: The Columbia Icefield is a massive ice sheet located in the heart of the Canadian Rockies. Visitors can take a guided tour of the icefield or walk on the Athabasca Glacier.

Jasper SkyTram: The Jasper SkyTram is a popular attraction that takes visitors to the top of Whistlers Mountain for stunning views of the park and surrounding mountains.

Miette Hot Springs: The Miette Hot Springs are the hottest mineral springs in the Canadian Rockies and are a popular spot for relaxing after a day of hiking or skiing.

Athabasca Falls: This powerful waterfall is one of the most popular attractions in Jasper National Park. Visitors can hike to several viewpoints to get a closer look at the falls and the surrounding canyon.

Wildlife viewing: Jasper National Park is home to a wide range of wildlife, including bears, elk, moose, bighorn sheep, and mountain goats. Visitors can go on a guided wildlife tour or explore the park on their own to spot these magnificent creatures.

Hiking: Jasper National Park has over 1,200 km of hiking trails, ranging from easy walks to challenging multi-day backpacking trips. Some popular hikes include the Sulphur Skyline Trail, the Valley of the Five Lakes Trail, and the Tonquin Valley.

Camping: Jasper National Park has several campgrounds that offer a range of camping options, from backcountry camping to RV camping with full amenities.

Skiing: In the winter, Jasper National Park is a popular destination for skiing and snowboarding. The park has several ski resorts, including Marmot Basin, which offers over 1,600 acres of skiable terrain.

Stargazing: Jasper National Park is one of the best places in the world for stargazing, thanks to its dark skies and lack of light pollution. Visitors can attend guided stargazing events or explore the park on their own to see the Milky Way and other celestial wonders.

Best Hikes and Trails:

Jasper National Park is home to several hiking trails, ranging from easy to challenging. Some of the popular hikes include the Bald Hills Trail, which offers stunning views of Maligne Lake and the surrounding mountains, and the Sulphur Skyline Trail, which takes hikers to the top of a mountain for panoramic views of the park. Other popular trails include the Valley of the Five Lakes Trail and the Wilcox Pass Trail.

Wildlife and Nature Watching:

Jasper National Park is home to various ranges of wildlife, including grizzly bears, black bears, elk, moose, wolves, and mountain goats. Visitors can observe these animals in their natural habitats by taking guided wildlife tours or driving along the park's scenic roads. The park is also home to several bird species, including bald eagles and ospreys.

Travel Tips

When visiting Jasper National Park, it is important to be prepared for the weather, as it can change quickly. Visitors should also be aware of the park's rules and regulations, including those related to wildlife and camping. It is also recommended that visitors bring bear spray when hiking or camping in the park. Additionally, visitors should be mindful of the park's Leave No Trace policy, which encourages visitors to minimize their impact on the environment.

One of the best things about Jasper National Park is its accessibility. With its close proximity to major cities and highways, it is easy to get to and navigate around.

However, visitors should still take the time to plan their trip ahead of time to ensure they make the most of their visit.

If you are planning a trip to Jasper National Park, it is important to research the various accommodation options available and book in advance to avoid disappointment. Whether you prefer the comfort of a hotel room or the ruggedness of camping, there are plenty of options to choose from.

When it comes to activities, hiking is one of the most popular ways to explore the park. There are several trails to choose from, ranging from short and easy walks to challenging multi-day hikes. Regardless of your fitness level, there is a trail that will suit your needs.

In addition to hiking, there are plenty of other activities to enjoy in Jasper National Park. Wildlife viewing is a popular pastime, with the park being home to a wide range of animals. Visitors can also enjoy fishing, boating, kayaking, and rafting on the park's many lakes and rivers. For those who prefer a more leisurely pace, there are several scenic drives to explore, including the famous Icefields Parkway.

One of the best things about Jasper National Park is the opportunity to disconnect from the hustle and bustle of everyday life and connect with nature. With its stunning scenery and abundant wildlife, it is the perfect place to relax, unwind, and recharge.

Overall, Jasper National Park is a truly special place that should be on every outdoor adventurer's bucket list. With its rich history, breathtaking landscapes, and endless opportunities for exploration, it is easy to see why it is one of the most popular national parks in Canada.

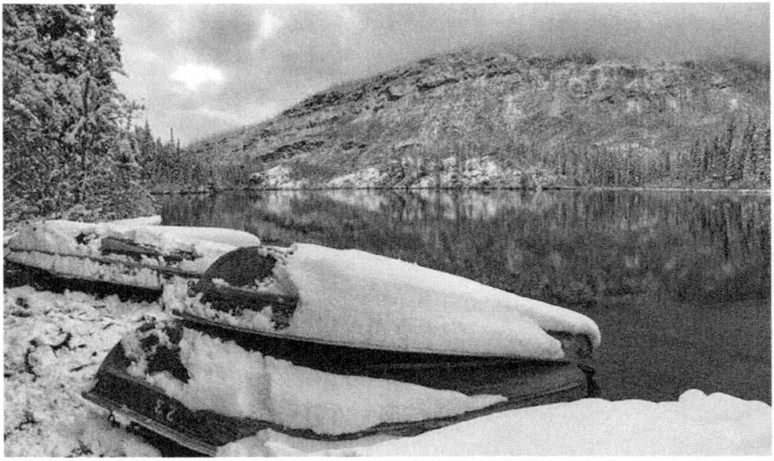

Chapter 5
Yoho National Park

Overview

Yoho National Park is located in the eastern part of British Columbia, Canada, and is one of the most stunning natural wonders in the country. The park was established in 1886 and is known for its dramatic mountain peaks, lush forests, crystal-clear lakes, and powerful waterfalls. Yoho National Park covers an area of over 1,300 square kilometers and is home to a diverse range of flora and fauna.

History and Geography

The name Yoho is derived from the Cree word "yoho," which means "awe and wonder." The park is situated in the western slopes of the Canadian Rocky Mountains and is bordered by Banff National Park to the east and Kootenay National Park to the south. The park's history dates back to the late 1800s when the Canadian Pacific Railway was being built. The railway company wanted to attract more tourists to the area and decided to establish a national park. Yoho National Park was officially created in 1886 and was the second national park to be established in Canada.

Getting There and Around

Yoho National Park is easily accessible by car from Banff, which is only a 30-minute drive away. The closest international airport is Calgary International Airport, which is about a two-hour drive from the park. Visitors can also take the train to the park's nearest town, Field, which is located just outside the park's boundaries.

Once inside the park, there are several options for getting around, including hiking, biking, and driving. The park has several well-maintained roads that provide access to some of the park's most popular attractions, such as Lake Louise and the Burgess Shale fossil beds.

Where to stay:

There are several options for accommodations within Yoho National Park, including campsites, cabins, and lodges. Some of the most popular places to stay include the

Cathedral Mountain Lodge, Emerald Lake Lodge, and the Lake O'Hara Lodge. Visitors can also camp at one of the park's several campgrounds, including the Kicking Horse and Takakkaw Falls campgrounds.

Popular Activities and Attractions

Here are some popular activities and attractions that visitors can enjoy:

Hiking: Yoho National Park has many hiking trails, from easy walks to strenuous hikes. Some of the popular hiking trails are the Iceline Trail, the Burgess Shale Fossil Beds, and the Lake O'Hara Alpine Circuit.

Lake Louise: While not technically in Yoho National Park, Lake Louise is a nearby attraction that is definitely worth visiting. The turquoise-colored lake is surrounded by mountains and is a popular spot for hiking and canoeing.

Takakkaw Falls: Takakkaw Falls is a magnificent waterfall that drops 302 meters (988 feet) into a gorge. It is one of the highest waterfalls in Canada and is easily accessible by car.

Emerald Lake: Emerald Lake is a beautiful glacial lake located in Yoho National Park. The lake is a popular spot for canoeing, hiking, and fishing.

Natural Bridge: The Natural Bridge is a rock formation that was created by the powerful Kicking Horse River. Visitors can walk across the bridge and enjoy the views of the river below.

Wapta Falls: Wapta Falls is a stunning waterfall that drops 30 meters (98 feet) into the Kicking Horse River. The falls are located a short hike from the parking area.

Spiral Tunnels: The Spiral Tunnels are a series of tunnels that were built to help trains navigate the steep terrain of the Rockies. Visitors can watch the trains as they pass through the tunnels.

Kicking Horse River: The Kicking Horse River is a popular spot for white-water rafting and kayaking. There are also many hiking trails along the river.

Burgess Shale Fossil Beds: The Burgess Shale Fossil Beds are a UNESCO World Heritage site located in Yoho

National Park. Visitors can take guided tours to learn about the many fossils that have been found there.

Mount Burgess: Mount Burgess is a popular spot for rock climbing and hiking. The mountain offers stunning views of the surrounding landscape.

Best hikes and trails:

Yoho National Park is known for its incredible hiking trails, which range from easy walks to challenging multi-day hikes. Some of the most popular hikes in the park include the Iceline Trail, which provides stunning views of the surrounding mountains and glaciers, and the Lake O'Hara Alpine Circuit, which is considered one of the most beautiful hikes in the world.

Wildlife and nature watching:

Yoho National Park has a diverse range of wildlife. Visitors can also spot several bird species, including bald eagles, ospreys, and great horned owls. The park's dense forests and pristine lakes provide ample opportunities for nature watching.

Travel Tips

When visiting Yoho National Park, it's important to come prepared for the changing weather conditions. The park's high elevation and mountainous terrain can lead to sudden changes in temperature and weather patterns. Visitors should also be aware of the park's wildlife and take precautions to avoid encounters with bears and other dangerous animals.

Additionally, visitors should ensure you pack plenty of water and snacks, as there are limited amenities within the park. Finally, visitors should make sure to follow Leave No Trace principles to help preserve the park's natural beauty for future generations.

Leave No Trace is an important principle to keep in mind when visiting Yoho National Park. Visitors should pack out all their trash and avoid leaving any trace of their presence in the park. This means being mindful of where you step and avoiding damaging any vegetation or wildlife habitat.

Another tip for visiting Yoho National Park is to plan ahead and make reservations for accommodations and activities.

The park is a popular destination, and accommodations can fill up quickly, especially during peak season. Planning ahead can help ensure that you get the most out of your visit.

It's also important to be aware of the park's rules and regulations. Visitors should familiarize themselves with the park's guidelines for camping, hiking, and wildlife viewing to ensure a safe and enjoyable visit.

Finally, visitors should take the time to learn about the park's history and natural features. The park offers several interpretive programs and guided tours, which can provide a deeper understanding of the park's ecology, geology, and cultural significance.

Yoho National Park is a must-visit destination for outdoor enthusiasts and nature lovers. Its stunning landscapes, diverse wildlife, and incredible hiking trails make it one of the most beautiful places in Canada. By following these tips and guidelines, visitors can have a safe and enjoyable experience while helping to preserve this natural wonder for future generations.

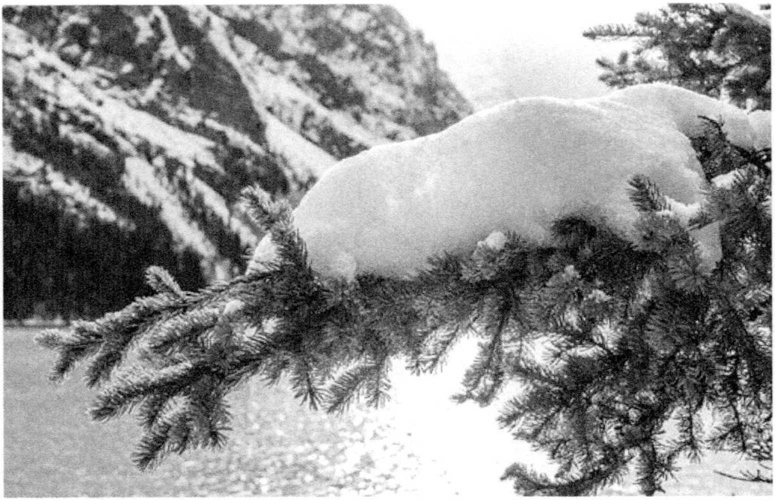

Chapter 6

Kootenay National Park

Overview

Kootenay National Park is a picturesque natural paradise located in British Columbia, Canada. This park is a part of the Canadian Rocky Mountains and boasts of several natural wonders that are worth exploring. It is a great destination for outdoor enthusiasts, wildlife enthusiasts, and those looking for a peaceful escape into nature.

History and Geography

The history of Kootenay National Park is closely linked to the history of the Canadian Pacific Railway, which was built in the late 19th century. The railway company wanted to attract tourists to the area, and thus, the idea of a national park was born. In 1920, the park was officially established as part of a system of national parks in Canada.

Kootenay National Park covers an area of 1,406 square kilometers and is situated in the southeastern region of British Columbia. The park is home to several natural features, including the Rocky Mountains, glaciers, rivers, waterfalls, and hot springs. It is also home to a diverse range of flora and fauna, including grizzly bears, elk, moose, and bighorn sheep.

Getting There and Around

Kootenay National Park is easily accessible by road, with Highway 93 running through the park. The park is located approximately 140 kilometers west of Calgary, Alberta, and 130 kilometers east of Golden, British Columbia. There are several shuttle services available that run from Calgary and Banff to the park.

Within the park, there are several scenic drives and hiking trails that allow visitors to explore the natural wonders of the park. The park also offers guided tours and interpretive programs for visitors who want to learn more about the park's history and geography.

Where to Stay

Kootenay National Park offers several accommodation options for visitors, including campgrounds, RV parks, and lodges. There are four campgrounds within the park, including Redstreak, Marble Canyon, McLeod Meadows, and Crooked Creek. These campgrounds offer both tent and RV camping facilities and provide basic amenities like toilets, showers, and fire pits.

For visitors who prefer more comfortable lodging, there are several lodges located within the park. These lodges offer a range of accommodations, from rustic cabins to luxurious suites. Some of the popular lodges include the Num-Ti-Jah Lodge, the Kootenay Park Lodge, and the Storm Mountain Lodge.

Popular Activities and Attractions

Kootenay National Park offers a range of activities for visitors to enjoy, including hiking, camping, wildlife watching, and hot spring soaking. One of the park's most popular attractions is the Radium Hot Springs, which is a natural hot spring that provides a relaxing soak in a beautiful setting. The hot springs are located on the park's western boundary and are open year-round.

Another popular attraction in the park is the Paint Pots, which are a series of colorful mineral pools located along the Vermilion River. The paint pots are a unique geological formation and are a great spot for a short hike and picnic.

Visitors can also explore the park's natural wonders by driving along the scenic Banff-Windermere Highway, which offers breathtaking views of the Rocky Mountains, glaciers, and waterfalls.

Best Hikes and Trails:

Kootenay National Park has several hiking trails that offer stunning views of the park's natural wonders. One of the park's best hikes is the Rockwall Trail, which is a multi-day hike that offers spectacular views of the park's alpine scenery. The trail is 55 kilometers long and takes approximately 3-5 days to complete.

Another popular hike in the park is the Stanley Glacier Trail, which is a moderate hike that offers stunning views of the Stanley Glacier and its surrounding mountains. The trail is 8.4 kilometers long and takes approximately 3-4 hours to complete.

Wildlife and Nature Watching:

Kootenay National Park is also home to a diverse range of wildlife. Visitors can watch wildlife from a safe distance and should never approach or feed wildlife.

The park is also home to several natural wonders, including glaciers, rivers, waterfalls, and hot springs. Visitors can explore these natural features and learn more about the park's unique geology and ecology.

Travel Tips

Bring appropriate clothing and gear for the weather and activities you plan to do.

Respect wildlife and maintain a safe distance from them.

Be prepared for changes in weather and temperature, especially at higher elevations.

Plan ahead and book accommodations and activities in advance, especially during peak season.

Follow park regulations and guidelines to help preserve the park's natural beauty for future generations.

In conclusion, Kootenay National Park is a must-visit destination for outdoor enthusiasts and nature lovers. With its stunning scenery, natural wonders, and diverse range of activities, the park offers something for everyone. Whether you're looking to relax in natural hot springs or to embark on a multi-day hiking adventure, Kootenay National Park is sure to leave a lasting impression on you.

Chapter 7

Glacier National Park

Overview

Glacier National Park is a stunningly beautiful and diverse national park located in British Columbia, Canada. It is part of the Canadian Rockies and is known for its snow-capped mountains, glaciers, alpine lakes, and vast wilderness areas. The park is home to a wide range of flora and fauna, including grizzly bears, mountain goats, and bighorn sheep.

The park is one of the largest in Canada and covers an area of over 1,349 square kilometers. The park also boasts more than 400 kilometers of hiking trails, which attract thousands of outdoor enthusiasts every year. The park is divided into two sections, with the Rogers Pass section to the east and the Illecillewaet section to the west.

History and Geography

Glacier National Park has a rich history, with evidence of human occupation dating back thousands of years. The park was established in 1886 as part of Canada's first national park system, which also included Banff and Yoho National Parks. The park was originally named Selkirk Mountains Park, but it was later renamed Glacier National Park due to the presence of glaciers in the area.

The park is located in the Columbia Mountains, a range of mountains that runs from northern Washington through British Columbia and into the Yukon Territory. The park is home to some of the highest peaks in the Canadian Rockies, including Mount Sir Donald, which stands at 3,284 meters.

Getting There and Around

Glacier National Park is easily accessible by car, with the Trans-Canada Highway running through the park. The park is located approximately 150 kilometers east of Kamloops and 300 kilometers west of Calgary. The nearest airport is located in Kamloops, and there are also bus services that operate to the park.

Once inside the park, there are a variety of transportation options available. Visitors can drive their own vehicles, take a shuttle bus, or hire a guide to explore the park. Hiking is also a popular way to explore the park, with a variety of trails suitable for all levels of experience.

Where to Stay

There are a variety of accommodation options available in and around Glacier National Park. The park has several campgrounds, including the Illecillewaet Campground and the Loop Brook Campground. These campgrounds offer a range of amenities, including fire pits, picnic tables, and washrooms.

For those who prefer more comfortable accommodations, there are several lodges and hotels located in the nearby towns of Revelstoke and Golden. These include the Glacier House Resort, the Sutton Place Hotel, and the Revelstoke Mountain Resort.

In conclusion, Glacier National Park is a must-visit destination for any outdoor adventurer looking to explore the natural wonders of Canada. With its rich history, diverse geography, and wide range of activities and accommodations, Glacier National Park has something for everyone.

Popular Activities

Glacier National Park is an outdoor adventurer's paradise, offering a wide range of activities for visitors to enjoy. Here are some of the most popular activities in the park:

Hiking: Glacier National Park boasts more than 400 kilometers of hiking trails, ranging from easy strolls to challenging alpine hikes. Some of the most popular trails in the park include the Abbott Ridge Trail, the Balu Pass Trail, and the Asulkan Valley Trail.

Mountaineering: The park is home to some of the highest peaks in the Canadian Rockies, making it a popular destination for mountaineers. Mount Sir Donald, the highest peak in the park, is a particularly challenging climb.

Skiing and Snowboarding: During the winter months, Glacier National Park is a popular destination for skiers and snowboarders. The park offers a range of terrain, from groomed runs to backcountry bowls.

Wildlife Viewing: In Glacier National Park, visitors can spot these animals by taking a wildlife viewing tour or by exploring the park's many hiking trails.

Fishing: The park's rivers and lakes offer some of the best fishing in British Columbia, with trout and salmon being the most common catches.

Camping: Glacier National Park has several campgrounds, offering visitors the opportunity to spend a night or two under the stars. The park's campgrounds offer a range of amenities, including fire pits, picnic tables, and washrooms.

Photography: With its stunning scenery and diverse wildlife, Glacier National Park is a photographer's dream. Visitors can capture the beauty of the park by taking a photography tour or by exploring the park's many hiking trails.

Glacier National Park offers a wide range of activities for visitors to enjoy, from hiking and mountaineering to skiing and wildlife viewing. With so much to see and do, the park is the ultimate destination for outdoor adventurers.

Attractions

Glacier National Park is home to some of the most stunning natural attractions in Canada. Here are some of the top attractions that visitors should not miss:

Rogers Pass: Rogers Pass is a mountain pass that cuts through the Selkirk Mountains, offering stunning views of the surrounding peaks. The pass is home to the Rogers Pass National Historic Site, which commemorates the construction of the Canadian Pacific Railway through the area.

Illecillewaet Glacier: Illecillewaet Glacier is a large glacier located in the park's northern section. Visitors can hike to the glacier's toe for an up-close look at its stunning blue ice.

Hemlock Grove Boardwalk: The Hemlock Grove Boardwalk is a short, easy trail that winds through an old-growth forest of Western Hemlock trees. The boardwalk is wheelchair accessible and offers a unique opportunity to explore the park's diverse flora and fauna.

Giant Cedars Boardwalk: The Giant Cedars Boardwalk is a short, easy trail that winds through a grove of ancient Western Red Cedar trees. The boardwalk offers a unique opportunity to see some of the park's oldest and largest trees up close.

Asulkan Valley: Asulkan Valley is a popular destination for hikers and mountaineers, offering stunning views of the surrounding peaks and glaciers. The valley is home to several backcountry campsites, making it a popular destination for multi-day hiking trips.

Glacier House: Glacier House is a historic hotel located in the park's western section, near the town of Revelstoke. The hotel was originally built in the late 1800s to serve as a stop for the Canadian Pacific Railway, and today it offers visitors a glimpse into the park's rich history.

Glacier Skywalk: The Glacier Skywalk is a glass-bottomed observation platform located in the park's southern section, offering stunning views of the surrounding mountains and valleys.

Glacier National Park is home to a wide range of natural attractions, from stunning mountain passes and glaciers to ancient forests and historic landmarks. By exploring these attractions, visitors can experience the park's beauty and learn about its rich history and ecology.

Travel Tips

If you're planning a trip to Glacier National Park, here are some travel tips to help you make the most of your visit:

Plan ahead: Glacier National Park is a popular destination, so it's important to plan ahead to ensure that you can secure the accommodations and activities that you want.

Dress in layers: The weather in Glacier National Park can be unpredictable, so it's a good idea to dress in layers so that you can adjust your clothing as needed.

Bring appropriate gear: If you're planning on hiking or mountaineering, make sure that you bring appropriate gear, including sturdy footwear, a backpack, and a map.

Be bear aware: Glacier National Park is home to grizzly bears and black bears, so it's important to be bear aware. This means carrying bear spray, making noise while hiking, and storing food properly.

Respect the environment: Glacier National Park is a protected area, so it's important to respect the environment by following Leave No Trace principles. This means packing out all trash and minimizing your impact on the natural environment.

Check for road closures: The Trans-Canada Highway, which runs through the park, can be subject to closures due to weather or other factors. Before heading out, be sure to check for road closures and plan your route accordingly.

Bring plenty of water and snacks: It's important to stay hydrated and fueled during your visit to Glacier National Park, so be sure to bring plenty of water and snacks.

Consider hiring a guide: If you're not familiar with the area, or if you're planning on engaging in more advanced activities like mountaineering, consider hiring a guide to help you navigate the park safely.

With a little planning and preparation, a trip to Glacier National Park can be a memorable and rewarding experience. By following these travel tips, you can ensure that you make the most of your visit to this stunningly beautiful park.

Chapter 8
Waterton Lakes National Park

Overview

Waterton Lakes National Park is a stunning natural wonder located in the southwestern part of Alberta, Canada, and is considered one of the most beautiful national parks in the country. Covering an area of over 500 square kilometers, the park is home to a variety of ecosystems, including forests, lakes, and grasslands. It is also home to an abundance of wildlife, including grizzly bears, moose, and bighorn sheep.

The park's most popular attraction is the Waterton Lakes, which are made up of three interconnected lakes: Upper Waterton Lake, Middle Waterton Lake, and Lower Waterton Lake. These lakes are surrounded by stunning mountains, including the towering Mount Cleveland, which is the highest peak in the park.

History and Geography

Waterton Lakes National Park has a rich history that dates back thousands of years. The area has been inhabited by indigenous peoples for over 10,000 years, and the Blackfoot tribe used the area as a hunting ground for buffalo. In the 1800s, European fur traders and explorers began to visit the area, and by the late 1800s, the Canadian government had established a national park there.

The park's geography is characterized by its mountains, lakes, and forests. The park is located at the intersection of the Rocky Mountains and the Great Plains, which gives it a unique mix of ecosystems. The park is also home to the Waterton-Glacier International Peace Park, which is a UNESCO World Heritage site and the first international peace park in the world.

Getting There and Around

Waterton Lakes National Park is located approximately 290 kilometers south of Calgary, Alberta, and is easily accessible by car. Visitors can also fly into the Calgary International Airport and rent a car to drive to the park.

Once in the park, visitors can get around by car, bike, or on foot. There are several scenic drives in the park, including the Akamina Parkway, which offers stunning views of the park's mountains and lakes. There are also several hiking trails in the park, ranging from easy walks to challenging multi-day hikes.

Where to Stay

There are several accommodation options in Waterton Lakes National Park, ranging from campsites to luxury lodges. The park has three campgrounds, including the Townsite Campground, which is located in the heart of the park and offers easy access to the park's amenities. There are also several backcountry campsites for visitors who want to experience the park's wilderness.

For visitors who prefer more comfortable accommodation, there are several lodges and hotels in the park, including the iconic Prince of Wales Hotel, which offers stunning views of the Waterton Lakes. There are also several vacation rentals and bed and breakfasts in the area.

Waterton Lakes National Park is a stunning natural wonder that offers visitors a unique mix of ecosystems and a rich history. Whether visitors want to hike, camp, or simply relax and take in the stunning views, Waterton Lakes National Park has something for everyone. With its easy accessibility, stunning scenery, and comfortable accommodation options, it is the perfect destination for outdoor adventurers looking to explore Canada's natural wonders.

Popular Activities

There are a variety of popular activities that visitors can enjoy when visiting Waterton Lakes National Park. Here are some examples:

Hiking: The park has over 200 kilometers of hiking trails, ranging from easy walks to challenging multi-day hikes. Some popular trails include the Crypt Lake Trail, which takes hikers through tunnels, over a waterfall, and along a narrow cliff ledge, and the Bear's Hump Trail, which offers stunning views of the park's mountains and lakes.

Boating and kayaking: The Waterton Lakes are a popular spot for boating and kayaking, and visitors can rent boats and kayaks from several local outfitters. The lakes are also home to several species of fish, including rainbow trout and cutthroat trout, making it a great spot for fishing enthusiasts.

Wildlife watching: Waterton Lakes National Park is home to a variety of wildlife. Visitors can take guided wildlife tours or explore the park on their own and keep an eye out for these magnificent creatures.

Scenic drives: The park has several scenic drives, including the Red Rock Parkway, which winds through the park's stunning red rock formations, and the Akamina Parkway, which offers breathtaking views of the park's mountains and lakes.

Photography: With its stunning natural beauty, Waterton Lakes National Park is a photographer's paradise. Visitors can capture stunning landscapes, wildlife, and wildflowers throughout the park.

Snowshoeing and cross-country skiing: In the winter months, visitors can enjoy snowshoeing and cross-country skiing on the park's trails. The park also offers guided snowshoe tours and equipment rentals.

These are just a few examples of the popular activities that visitors can enjoy when exploring Waterton Lakes National Park. With its diverse landscapes and abundance of wildlife, there is no shortage of things to do and see in this beautiful park.

Attractions

Waterton Lakes National Park is full of breathtaking natural wonders and stunning landscapes that make it an incredible destination for outdoor enthusiasts. Here are some of the top attractions and must-see sights in the park:

Waterton Lakes: The park's namesake lakes are a top attraction, and visitors can explore them by boat, kayak, or canoe. The lakes are surrounded by towering mountains and offer stunning views in every direction.

Prince of Wales Hotel: This iconic hotel is a must-see attraction in the park, with its grand architecture and stunning views of the Waterton Lakes. Visitors can enjoy a meal or a drink in the hotel's restaurant, or simply take in the views from the terrace.

Cameron Falls: This picturesque waterfall is a popular spot for photos and is located just a short walk from the park's townsite. The falls are surrounded by lush vegetation and offer a peaceful retreat for visitors.

Crypt Lake Trail: This challenging hike is one of the most popular in the park, and takes hikers through tunnels, over a waterfall, and along a narrow cliff ledge. The trail offers stunning views of the park's mountains and lakes, and is a must-do for adventurous hikers.

Red Rock Canyon: This striking red rock formation is a popular spot for photos and offers a unique contrast to the park's lush green forests and blue lakes. Visitors can walk along the canyon floor or hike up to a viewpoint for a bird's eye view.

Bison Paddock Loop Road: This scenic drive takes visitors through a paddock where bison roam freely. Visitors can watch these magnificent creatures graze and roam in their natural habitat, making it a popular spot for wildlife watching.

These are just a few of the many attractions and must-see sights in Waterton Lakes National Park. With its stunning natural beauty and diverse landscapes, there is always something new and exciting to discover in this incredible park.

Travel Tips

If you're planning a visit to Waterton Lakes National Park, here are some travel tips to help you make the most of your trip:

Plan ahead: The park can be busy during peak season, so it's a good idea to plan ahead and make reservations for accommodations, tours, and activities in advance.

Dress for the weather: The weather in Waterton Lakes National Park can be unpredictable, so it's important to dress in layers and bring appropriate gear for outdoor activities. Make sure to check the weather forecast before you go and pack accordingly.

Bring bear spray: The park is home to both grizzly and black bears, so it's important to carry bear spray with you when hiking or exploring the park. Bear spray can be purchased or rented from several local outfitters.

Respect wildlife: Waterton Lakes National Park is home to a variety of wildlife, and it's important to respect their natural habitat and keep a safe distance. Always give wildlife plenty of space and never approach or feed them.

Stay on designated trails: The park has over 200 kilometers of hiking trails, and it's important to stay on designated trails to protect the park's fragile ecosystems. Follow the park's Leave No Trace principles and pack out all trash and waste.

Check for park updates: Conditions in the park can change quickly, so it's important to check for updates on road closures, trail conditions, and wildlife sightings before you go. The park's website and social media pages are great resources for up-to-date information.

By following these travel tips, you can help ensure a safe and enjoyable visit to Waterton Lakes National Park. With its stunning natural beauty and diverse landscapes, it's sure to be an unforgettable experience for outdoor enthusiasts of all ages.

Chapter 9

Wood Buffalo National Park

Overview

Wood Buffalo National Park is known as the largest national park in Canada, spanning over 44,807 square kilometers of boreal forest and grasslands. It is located in the northeastern part of Alberta and the southern part of the Northwest Territories. Established in 1922, the park was created to protect the last remaining herd of wood bison, which at the time was on the brink of extinction.

Apart from the wood bison, the park is also home to other iconic Canadian wildlife such as grizzly bears, moose, wolves, and a variety of bird species. The park also boasts stunning natural features such as the world's largest freshwater delta, the Peace-Athabasca Delta, and the world's largest inland delta, the Slave River Delta.

History and Geography

Wood Buffalo National Park has a rich history dating back to the indigenous peoples who have lived in the area for thousands of years. The park is located on the traditional territories of the Dene Tha' First Nation and other indigenous groups.

In the early 1900s, the park was established to protect the wood bison population from overhunting and habitat destruction. The park was later expanded in the 1920s to include the Peace-Athabasca Delta and the Slave River Delta.

Geographically, the park is situated on the Canadian Shield and consists of a mix of boreal forest, wetlands, and grasslands. The park's terrain is characterized by rolling hills, deep valleys, and large river systems such as the Peace and Athabasca Rivers.

Getting There and Around

Wood Buffalo National Park is a remote location, and getting there can be a challenge. The closest major city is Fort McMurray, which is approximately 200 kilometers away. The park can be accessed via Highway 5, which runs through the park's southern border.

There are several ways to get around the park, including hiking trails, canoe routes, and driving tours. The park has several campgrounds and backcountry camping options, allowing visitors to stay in the park and explore its beauty at their own pace.

Where to Stay

There are several options for visitors looking to stay in or near Wood Buffalo National Park. The park has several campgrounds, including Pine Lake, Twin Falls, and Peace Point, which offer basic amenities such as fire pits and picnic tables. There are also several backcountry camping options for visitors looking to explore the park's remote wilderness.

For those who prefer more comfortable accommodations, there are several lodges and hotels in the nearby town of Fort McMurray. These accommodations offer a range of amenities, including restaurants, swimming pools, and guided tours of the park.

Wood Buffalo National Park is a unique and breathtaking destination for outdoor adventurers looking to explore Canada's natural wonders. With its rich history, stunning natural features, and abundant wildlife, it is a must-visit destination for anyone interested in experiencing the beauty of the Canadian wilderness.

Popular Activities

Wood Buffalo National Park offers visitors a wide range of activities to enjoy, from hiking and wildlife viewing to camping and canoeing. Here are some of the most popular activities in the park:

Wildlife viewing: The Park is home to a variety of wildlife, including the world's largest free-roaming herd of wood bison. Visitors can also spot other iconic Canadian animals, such as grizzly bears, moose, wolves, and bald eagles.

Hiking: The park has several hiking trails of varying difficulty, ranging from short nature walks to multi-day backcountry trips. Some of the most popular hikes include the Pine Lake Trail and the Salt River Trail.

Canoeing and kayaking: With its numerous rivers and lakes, Wood Buffalo National Park is a great destination for canoeing and kayaking. The park offers several canoe routes of varying length and difficulty, including the Peace River and the Slave River.

Camping: The park has several campgrounds and backcountry camping options for visitors looking to stay in the park. The campgrounds offer basic amenities such as fire pits and picnic tables, while backcountry camping allows visitors to explore the park's remote wilderness.

Fishing: The park is home to several species of fish, including northern pike and walleye. Fishing is allowed in designated areas, and visitors must have a valid fishing license.

Snowmobiling: In the winter months, the park's snow-covered terrain is a popular destination for snowmobiling. Visitors can explore the park's trails and frozen lakes, taking in the winter wonderland scenery.

In addition to these activities, the park also offers guided tours, interpretive programs, and educational activities for visitors of all ages. With so much to see and do, Wood Buffalo National Park is a destination that offers something for everyone.

Attractions

Wood Buffalo National Park offers visitors a wide variety of attractions to explore and experience. Here are some of the top attractions in the park:

The Wood Bison: The park is home to the world's largest free-roaming herd of wood bison. Visitors can watch these majestic animals roam freely in their natural habitat, and learn about the conservation efforts to protect this species.

The Peace-Athabasca Delta: The park is home to the world's largest freshwater delta, the Peace-Athabasca Delta. Visitors can explore this unique ecosystem, which supports a diverse range of wildlife and plant species.

The Slave River Delta: The park is also home to the world's largest inland delta, the Slave River Delta. Visitors can paddle through this expansive wetland, taking in the beautiful scenery and spotting a variety of birds and wildlife.

Salt Plains: The park's salt plains are a unique geological feature, created by ancient sea beds that have been uplifted and exposed to the elements. Visitors can walk on the crunchy salt crystals and learn about the history of the area.

Northern Lights: Wood Buffalo National Park is a prime location to view the northern lights, also known as the aurora borealis. Visitors can marvel at the dazzling light show in the night sky, a truly unforgettable experience.

Wildflowers: In the summer months, the park's meadows are carpeted with wildflowers, including lupines, fireweed, and Indian paintbrush. Visitors can take a leisurely stroll or hike through these beautiful blooms, taking in the stunning colors and fragrances.

Fort Smith: Just outside the park, the town of Fort Smith offers a variety of cultural attractions, including the Northern Life Museum and Cultural Centre, which showcases the history and culture of the area's indigenous peoples.

With so many unique and breathtaking attractions, Wood Buffalo National Park is a destination that offers visitors a truly unforgettable experience.

Travel Tips

If you're planning a trip to Wood Buffalo National Park, here are some travel tips to help you make the most of your visit:

Plan ahead: Wood Buffalo National Park is a remote and isolated destination, so it's important to plan ahead and be prepared for the trip. Make sure to check the park's website for current conditions, park regulations, and any necessary permits or reservations.

Be wildlife-aware: The park is home to a variety of wildlife, including bears, wolves, and bison. It's important to follow the park's guidelines for wildlife safety, such as carrying bear spray and making noise while hiking.

Pack appropriately: The park's weather can be unpredictable, with cold temperatures and sudden storms possible at any time of year. Be sure to pack warm clothing, rain gear, and sturdy footwear for hiking.

Bring your own supplies: The park is remote and isolated, with limited services available. Be sure to bring your own food, water, and other supplies, and plan to pack out any garbage or waste.

Respect the park's ecosystem: Wood Buffalo National Park is a fragile ecosystem, and it's important to minimize your impact on the environment. Follow Leave No Trace principles, such as staying on designated trails and packing out all garbage.

Consider a guided tour: The park offers a variety of guided tours and interpretive programs, which can provide valuable insights into the park's ecology and history.

Have a backup plan: The park's remote location and unpredictable weather can sometimes cause unexpected changes to travel plans. Have a backup plan in case of inclement weather or other unforeseen circumstances.

By following these travel tips, you can ensure a safe and enjoyable trip to Wood Buffalo National Park, and make the most of your experience in this unique and breathtaking destination.

Chapter 10
Prince Albert National Park

Overview

Prince Albert National Park is one of Canada's natural wonders, located in the province of Saskatchewan. It covers an area of about 3,875 square kilometers, making it the third-largest national park in the province. The park is home to diverse ecosystems, including boreal forests, sand dunes, and lakes, providing a wide range of recreational activities for outdoor adventurers.

Visitors can explore the park's many hiking trails, go canoeing, fishing, camping, wildlife watching, and much more. The park's stunning scenery and natural beauty make it a must-visit destination for anyone looking to experience Canada's great outdoors.

History and Geography

Prince Albert National Park was established in 1927, primarily to protect the park's wildlife and natural habitats. The park's location, between the northern boreal forest and southern grasslands, makes it a unique area, providing a diverse range of flora and fauna.

The park's most prominent geographical feature is the Waskesiu Lake, which is the park's largest lake. The lake is surrounded by white sandy beaches and crystal-clear waters, making it a popular spot for swimming, boating, and fishing. Other geographical features in the park include the sand dunes, boreal forests, and rolling hills.

Getting There and Around

The park is located about 200 km north of Saskatoon and can be accessed by car. Visitors can drive to the park from Saskatoon via the highway or take a bus to the town of Prince Albert, where they can rent a car to drive to the park. There are also shuttle services available from Saskatoon that can transport visitors to the park.

Once inside the park, visitors can explore the park's many hiking trails by foot or rent a bike from one of the many rental shops in the park. Canoes, kayaks, and motorboats are also available for rent, allowing visitors to explore the park's many lakes and waterways.

Where to Stay

There are many accommodation options available for visitors to Prince Albert National Park. Visitors can choose from campsites, rustic cabins, lodges, and hotels, depending on their budget and preferences.

For those looking to camp, the park has several campgrounds, including the Beaver Glen Campground, the Waskesiu Lake Campground, and the Paignton Beach Campground. These campsites offer a range of amenities, including fire pits, picnic tables, and washrooms.

For those looking for a more luxurious experience, the park has several lodges and hotels, including the Waskesiu Lake Lodge, Elk Ridge Resort, and the Hawood Inn. These accommodations offer a range of amenities, including restaurants, indoor pools, and spas, making them perfect for those looking to relax and unwind after a long day of outdoor activities.

Prince Albert National Park is a must-visit destination for anyone looking to explore Canada's natural wonders. With its diverse ecosystems, stunning scenery, and a range of recreational activities, the park offers something for everyone. Visitors should plan ahead by knowing about the history and geography of the park, how to get there and around, and where to stay. By doing so, visitors can ensure that they have an unforgettable experience exploring one of Canada's most beautiful national parks.

Popular Activities

Prince Albert National Park offers a variety of activities for visitors to enjoy. Here are some of the popular activities:

Hiking: The park has over 150 kilometers of hiking trails that cater to all levels of hikers. Some of the popular trails include the Mud Creek Trail, the Narrows Trail, and the Boundary Bog Trail.

Canoeing and Kayaking: Visitors can rent canoes or kayaks to explore the park's numerous lakes and waterways. The

Waskesiu Lake is a popular spot for canoeing and kayaking.

Wildlife Watching: The park is home to a variety of wildlife, including moose, elk, black bears, and wolves. Visitors can observe these animals in their natural habitat from a safe distance.

Fishing: The park has over 40 lakes, offering excellent fishing opportunities for visitors. Some of the common fish species found in the park's lakes include walleye, northern pike, and lake trout.

Swimming: The park has several beaches, including the Main Beach at Waskesiu Lake, where visitors can swim and enjoy the warm waters.

Biking: The park has several bike trails that cater to all skill levels, including the Lakeshore Trail, which offers scenic views of the Waskesiu Lake.

Golfing: The park has two golf courses, including the Elk Ridge Resort Golf Course and the Waskesiu Golf Course, which offer challenging courses surrounded by stunning scenery.

Winter Activities: During the winter months, visitors can enjoy activities such as cross-country skiing, snowshoeing, and ice fishing.

These are just some of the popular activities that visitors can enjoy at Prince Albert National Park. With so much to see and do, the park offers endless opportunities for outdoor adventure.

Attractions

Prince Albert National Park has a variety of natural and cultural attractions that visitors can explore. Here are some of the top attractions:

Waskesiu Lake: The park's largest lake is a popular attraction for visitors, offering a range of recreational activities such as swimming, boating, and fishing.

Grey Owl's Cabin: Visitors can take a guided tour to Grey Owl's Cabin, which is located on the shores of Ajawaan Lake. The cabin is where the famous Canadian conservationist, Grey Owl, lived in the 1930s.

Beaver Creek Conservation Area: This area offers visitors a chance to see beavers in their natural habitat. Visitors can take a guided tour to learn more about these fascinating animals and their habitat.

The Narrows: This is a narrow channel that connects Waskesiu Lake and Kingsmere Lake. Visitors can take a boat tour to explore the area and see the beautiful scenery.

The Boreal Trail: This 120-kilometer trail offers visitors an opportunity to explore the boreal forest and see the park's diverse wildlife.

Elk Range: This area is home to a large population of elk, and visitors can take guided tours to see these magnificent animals up close.

The Megisan Lake Trail: This trail offers stunning views of the park's sand dunes and the surrounding landscape.

The Saskatchewan River Delta: Visitors can take a boat tour to explore the delta and see the many species of birds and other wildlife that call it home.

These are just a few of the many attractions that visitors can explore at Prince Albert National Park. With its diverse natural and cultural attractions, the park offers something for everyone.

Travel Tips

Here are some travel tips for visitors to Prince Albert National Park:

Plan ahead: Before visiting the park, it's important to plan ahead. Check the park's website for information on park rules and regulations, weather conditions, and road closures.

Pack appropriately: Depending on the time of year you are visiting, it's important to pack appropriate clothing and gear. For example, during the summer months, bring sunscreen, a hat, and insect repellent, while in winter, pack warm clothing and boots.

Stay on marked trails: To protect the park's delicate ecosystem, it's important to stay on marked trails and follow park regulations.

Respect wildlife: While the park is home to a variety of wildlife, it's important to observe these animals from a safe distance and not disturb them in their natural habitat.

Carry bear spray: It's always a good idea to carry bear spray while hiking or camping in the park, as black bears are common in the area.

Book accommodations in advance: Accommodations in the park can fill up quickly, especially during peak season. It's recommended to book accommodations in advance to avoid disappointment.

Bring your own food and water: While the park has restaurants and cafes, it's always a good idea to bring your own food and water, especially if you plan to explore the park's trails and backcountry.

Respect other visitors: It's important to respect other visitors by keeping noise levels down and following park rules and regulations.

By following these travel tips, visitors can ensure a safe and enjoyable experience in Prince Albert National Park.

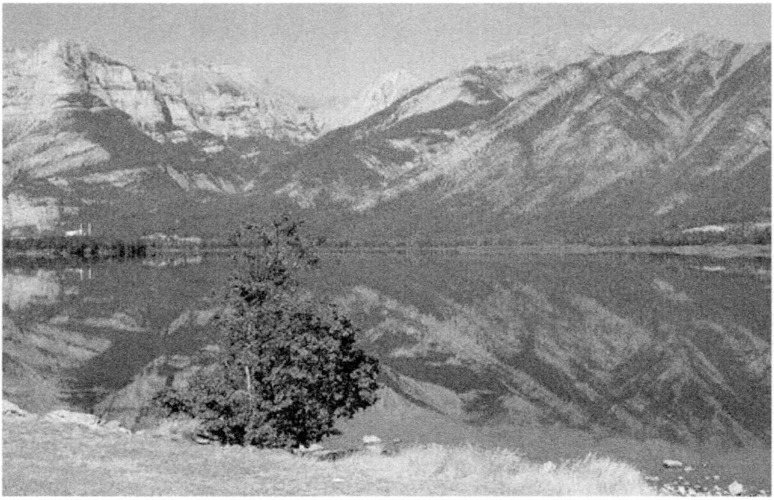

Chapter 11
Fundy National Park

Overview

Fundy National Park is a natural wonder located in the province of New Brunswick, Canada. The park is well-known for its stunning and diverse landscapes, including forests, beaches, waterfalls, and cliffs, as well as its rich wildlife and plant species.

Visitors can explore the park's natural beauty by hiking, camping, fishing, swimming, and boating. Fundy National Park is also renowned for its unique geological formations, such as the world's highest tides, which can reach up to 16 meters in height.

History and Geography

Fundy National Park was established in 1948 and covers an area of 206 square kilometers. The park is situated on the Bay of Fundy, a large tidal bay that stretches between New Brunswick and Nova Scotia. The park's terrain is rugged and hilly, with elevations ranging from sea level to over 300 meters.

The park's unique geology is a result of its location on the edge of the Appalachian Mountains and its exposure to the powerful tides of the Bay of Fundy. The park's forests are predominantly composed of maple, birch, and spruce trees, and are home to a diverse range of wildlife, including moose, black bears, beavers, and otters.

Getting There and Around

Fundy National Park is located approximately two hours from both Fredericton and Moncton, the two largest cities in New Brunswick. Visitors can travel to the park by car or public transportation. The nearest airport is in Moncton, which offers flights to several major Canadian cities. Once inside the park, visitors can explore the park's attractions by foot, bicycle, or car. The park has several hiking trails, ranging from short nature walks to multi-day backcountry hikes. The park also offers guided tours and interpretive programs for visitors.

Where to Stay

Fundy National Park offers a range of accommodation options for visitors, including campsites, yurts, and cabins. The park's campgrounds are equipped with amenities such as fire pits, picnic tables, and washrooms. Visitors can also choose to stay in one of the park's yurts, which offer a unique glamping experience with comfortable beds, heaters, and electricity.

For those seeking a more luxurious experience, the park also has several cabins and lodges, which offer amenities such as hot tubs, fireplaces, and fully equipped kitchens. Additionally, the park offers several dining options, including a restaurant and a cafe, as well as a general store for supplies and souvenirs.

Popular Activities

Fundy National Park offers a plethora of outdoor activities that cater to different interests and abilities. Some of the most popular activities include:

Hiking: The park features over 100 kilometers of hiking trails that range from easy walks to challenging multi-day hikes. The trails take visitors through forests, rivers, and mountains, offering breathtaking views and opportunities to spot wildlife.

Mountain biking: Fundy National Park has over 30 kilometers of biking trails, with varying difficulty levels. The trails take visitors through diverse terrain, including forests, meadows, and rocky ridges.

Kayaking and canoeing: Visitors can explore the park's rivers and lakes by renting kayaks and canoes. The park offers guided tours, as well as self-guided options, for visitors who prefer to explore on their own.

Beaches and swimming: The park has two supervised beaches, one of which is on the Bay of Fundy, and the other on a freshwater lake. Both beaches are perfect for swimming, sunbathing, and relaxing.

Wildlife watching: The park is home to several species of wildlife, including moose, deer, black bears, and coyotes. Visitors can spot these animals on hikes or join guided wildlife tours.

Attractions

Hopewell Rocks: Located about 45 minutes from the park, the Hopewell Rocks are a must-visit attraction. The rocks are tall, flowerpot-shaped formations that have been carved by the powerful tides of the Bay of Fundy. Visitors can walk on the ocean floor during low tide and admire the impressive rock formations.

Fundy Trail Parkway: The Fundy Trail Parkway is a scenic drive that stretches along the Bay of Fundy coastline. The drive takes visitors through breathtaking vistas and offers opportunities for hiking, biking, and picnicking.

Fundy Tidal Interpretive Centre: The interpretive center is located within the park and provides information about the tides of the Bay of Fundy. Visitors can watch a 3D movie, visit the interactive exhibits, and learn about the unique ecosystem of the area.

Mary's Point Bird Sanctuary: Located near the park, the bird sanctuary is a popular spot for bird watching. Visitors can observe different species of birds, including sandpipers and plovers, during their migration.

Travel Tips

Plan ahead: It's essential to plan your visit to Fundy National Park, especially during the high season (June to September). Book accommodation and activities in advance to avoid disappointment.

Dress appropriately: The weather in Fundy National Park can be unpredictable, and visitors should come prepared for different conditions. Dress in layers, bring waterproof clothing, and wear sturdy footwear.

Respect the wildlife: Visitors should always keep a safe distance from the park's wildlife and avoid feeding them. Feeding wildlife can cause them to become aggressive and dependent on humans.

Follow Leave No Trace principles: Visitors should always pack out what they pack in and leave the park as they found it. Littering and disturbing natural features can damage the park's delicate ecosystem.

Be prepared for the tides: Visitors should always check the tide schedule and plan their activities accordingly. The tides can rise and fall quickly, and visitors should avoid getting stranded or caught by the rising waters.

Chapter 12

Cape Breton Highlands National Park

Overview

Cape Breton Highlands National Park is a natural wonderland located on the northern tip of Cape Breton Island in Nova Scotia, Canada. This park covers an area of approximately 950 square kilometers and was established in 1936 as Canada's 10th national park. The park boasts stunning highlands, a rugged coastline, and diverse wildlife, making it an ideal destination for outdoor adventurers.

The park is home to a diverse range of ecosystems, from boreal forests to tundra-like landscapes. Visitors can explore the park's various trails and experience the breathtaking views from the many scenic lookouts. Some of the most popular trails include the Skyline Trail, the Franey Trail, and the Coastal Trail.

History and Geography

Cape Breton Highlands National Park is located on the northeastern tip of Nova Scotia, Canada. The park is situated on a high plateau, which rises to over 1,200 meters above sea level, providing breathtaking views of the Gulf of St. Lawrence and the Atlantic Ocean.

The park's history dates back to the early 1900s when conservationists began advocating for the preservation of the region's unique natural beauty. In 1936, the park was officially established, and since then, it has become a popular destination for outdoor enthusiasts from around the world.

Getting There and Around

Visitors can access Cape Breton Highlands National Park by road, air, or sea. The park is approximately a four-hour drive from Halifax, the capital city of Nova Scotia. Visitors can also fly into the nearby Sydney Airport and rent a car to reach the park.

Once inside the park, visitors can explore the various attractions by car, bike, or on foot. There are several parking areas throughout the park, making it easy to access the different hiking trails and scenic lookouts. The Cabot Trail, a famous scenic drive that winds through the park, is a must-see for visitors to the area.

Where to Stay

Cape Breton Highlands National Park offers a range of accommodation options to suit every budget and preference. Visitors can choose to stay at one of the park's campgrounds, which offer both serviced and unserviced sites. There are also several backcountry camping options for those looking for a more rugged experience.

For those who prefer more comfortable accommodations, there are several lodges and inns located within the park. The Keltic Lodge at the Highlands, located on the Cabot Trail, offers luxurious accommodations and stunning views of the ocean. The Chéticamp Campground and Cabins, located on the park's western side, offers cozy cabins and traditional campsites.

Cape Breton Highlands National Park is a natural wonder that offers visitors the opportunity to experience the beauty and diversity of the Canadian wilderness. With its stunning landscapes, diverse wildlife, and range of activities and accommodations, this park is the ultimate destination for outdoor adventurers. Whether hiking the trails, exploring the coastline, or simply taking in the breathtaking views, visitors are sure to have an unforgettable experience at Cape Breton Highlands National Park.

Popular Attractions

Cape Breton Highlands National Park is home to many popular attractions that draw visitors from around the world. Some of the most popular attractions include:

Skyline Trail: The Skyline Trail is a must-visit destination within the park. The trail offers stunning views of the highlands, the Gulf of St. Lawrence, and the Cabot Trail. It is a relatively easy hike and is approximately 7.5 km in length.

Cabot Trail: The Cabot Trail is a scenic drive that winds its way through Cape Breton Highlands National Park. The route offers stunning views of the coast and the highlands and is a popular destination for photographers.

Middle Head Trail: The Middle Head Trail is a popular hiking trail that offers stunning views of the coastline and the Atlantic Ocean. It is a relatively easy hike and is approximately 4 km in length.

Fishing: The park is home to several streams and rivers that offer excellent fishing opportunities for trout, salmon, and other freshwater fish.

Wildlife Viewing: Cape Breton Highlands National Park has a diverse range of wildlife, including moose, black bears, bald eagles, and whales. Visitors can take guided tours or explore on their own to view the wildlife in their natural habitat.

Beaches: The park is home to several beautiful beaches, including Ingonish Beach and Black Brook Beach. These beaches offer visitors the opportunity to swim, sunbathe, and enjoy the stunning coastal views.

Golfing: The park is home to two golf courses, the Highlands Links Golf Course and the Le Portage Golf

Club. These courses offer stunning views of the highlands and the coast and are a must-visit destination for golfers.

Cape Breton Highlands National Park offers visitors a range of attractions that cater to every interest and activity level. From hiking the trails and taking in the stunning views to fishing, wildlife viewing, and golfing, there is something for everyone to enjoy at this natural wonderland.

Activities

Cape Breton Highlands National Park offers visitors a range of activities that cater to every interest and ability level. Whether visitors are looking for a challenging hike, a leisurely stroll, or a scenic drive, the park has something to offer everyone. Here are some of the most popular activities:

Hiking: The park is home to over 20 hiking trails, ranging from easy strolls to challenging hikes. Some of the most popular trails include the Skyline Trail, the Franey Trail, and the Coastal Trail.

Biking: The park has several biking trails that offer visitors a chance to explore the park on two wheels. The Cabot

Trail is a popular destination for road cycling, while the Celtic Shores Coastal Trail is a great option for mountain biking.

Wildlife Viewing: The park is home to a diverse range of wildlife, including moose, black bears, bald eagles, and whales. Visitors can take guided tours or explore on their own to view the wildlife in their natural habitat.

Fishing: The park is home to several streams and rivers that offer excellent fishing opportunities for trout, salmon, and other freshwater fish.

Swimming: Visitors can enjoy swimming at several beaches in the park, including Ingonish Beach and Black Brook Beach.

Camping: The park has several campgrounds that offer both serviced and unserviced sites. Visitors can choose from front-country or backcountry camping options.

Golfing: The park is home to two golf courses, the Highlands Links Golf Course and the Le Portage Golf Club. These courses offer stunning views of the highlands and the coast and are a must-visit destination for golfers.

Snowshoeing and Cross-Country Skiing: During the winter months, visitors can enjoy snowshoeing and cross-country skiing on several trails in the park.

Cape Breton Highlands National Park offers visitors a range of activities that cater to every interest and ability level. From hiking and biking to wildlife viewing, fishing, and camping, there is something for everyone to enjoy at this natural wonderland.

Travel Tips

Traveling to Cape Breton Highlands National Park can be an incredible experience, but it's important to plan ahead and be prepared. Here are some travel tips to help make your trip to the park a success:

Plan ahead: Make sure to research the park and plan your itinerary ahead of time. This will help ensure that you get the most out of your visit and don't miss any must-see attractions.

Check the weather: Cape Breton Highlands National Park experiences a range of weather conditions, from warm summers to cold winters. Check the weather forecast before your trip and pack accordingly.

Dress appropriately: Whether you're hiking or simply exploring the park, it's important to dress appropriately for the weather and activity. Wear sturdy footwear, dress in layers, and bring rain gear if necessary.

Bring binoculars: Cape Breton Highlands National Park is home to a diverse range of wildlife, and bringing binoculars can help you spot animals from a safe distance.

Bring a map: While the park has good signage, it's still a good idea to bring a map to ensure you don't get lost on the trails.

Pack snacks and water: It's important to stay hydrated and fueled while exploring the park, so make sure to bring plenty of water and snacks.

Respect the wildlife: While it's exciting to see wildlife up close, it's important to respect their space and observe them from a safe distance. Don't approach or feed wild animals, and follow any wildlife viewing guidelines provided by park staff.

Leave no trace: When exploring the park, make sure to pack out any trash and leave the natural environment as you found it.

Book accommodations in advance: If you plan on staying in the park or nearby, make sure to book your accommodations in advance as they can fill up quickly, especially during peak season.

Following these travel tips can help ensure a safe and enjoyable trip to Cape Breton Highlands National Park. Plan ahead, dress appropriately, bring the right gear, and respect the wildlife and natural environment, and you're sure to have a memorable experience in this natural wonderland.

Chapter 13

Activities in the National Parks

Canada's National Parks are an adventurer's paradise, with a wide range of activities to suit all types of outdoor enthusiasts. Whether you're a thrill-seeker looking for an adrenaline rush or a nature lover seeking a peaceful escape, the parks have something for everyone. In this chapter, we'll explore the major activities available in Canada's National Parks.

Hiking

Hiking is one of the most popular activities in Canada's National Parks. With over 100,000 kilometers of trails, hikers can explore the natural beauty of the parks, from rugged mountains to peaceful meadows. Each park has its own unique trails, ranging from easy walks to challenging multi-day hikes.

Iin Banff National Park, you can hike the popular Plain of Six Glaciers Trail, which offers stunning views of the glaciers and surrounding mountains. In Gros Morne

National Park, you can hike the Long Range Traverse, a challenging 35-kilometer trail that takes you through the park's rugged backcountry.

Wildlife Viewing

Canada's National Parks are home to a diverse range of wildlife, including bears, moose, elk, and wolves. Wildlife viewing is a popular activity in the parks, and many offer guided tours or educational programs to help visitors learn about the animals and their habitats. For example, in Jasper National Park, you can take a guided wildlife tour and spot bighorn sheep, mountain goats, and grizzly bears. In the Pacific Rim National Park Reserve, you can watch the gray whales as they migrate along the coast.

Camping

Camping is a quintessential Canadian experience, and the National Parks offer some of the best camping opportunities in the country. From tent camping to RV camping, there are options for every type of camper. Many of the parks have designated campgrounds, with amenities like fire pits, picnic tables, and washrooms. For example, in

Fundy National Park, you can camp in the woods near the Bay of Fundy, where you can witness the world's highest tides. In Waterton Lakes National Park, you can camp at the Crandell Mountain Campground and wake up to stunning views of the Rocky Mountains.

Canoeing and Kayaking

Canada's National Parks are home to some of the most picturesque lakes and rivers in the world, making canoeing and kayaking a popular activity. Paddling through the parks' waterways offers a unique perspective on the surrounding landscape and provides opportunities for wildlife viewing. For example, in Algonquin Provincial Park, you can canoe the park's network of lakes and rivers and camp on the shores. In Kejimkujik National Park, you can paddle the Mersey River and explore the park's lush forests and wetlands.

Winter Sports

Many of Canada's National Parks are open year-round, offering a range of winter activities for visitors. From skiing and snowshoeing to ice skating and ice fishing, there's something for everyone to enjoy. For example, in Banff National Park, you can hit the slopes at one of the park's three ski resorts, or snowshoe through the pristine wilderness. In Riding Mountain National Park, you can skate on the frozen Clear Lake and watch the northern lights dance across the sky.

Canada's National Parks offer a diverse range of activities for outdoor adventurers, from hiking and wildlife viewing to camping and winter sports. With so many options to choose from, visitors can customize their experience to suit their interests and abilities.

Chapter 14

Beyond the National Parks

Other Natural Attractions

In addition to the national parks, Canada boasts a plethora of other natural wonders that are worth exploring for outdoor enthusiasts. From rugged coastlines to majestic mountains, Canada's diverse landscapes offer something for everyone.

One such attraction is the Cabot Trail, a 300-kilometer scenic drive that winds through Cape Breton Highlands National Park in Nova Scotia. The trail takes visitors on a journey through quaint fishing villages, rugged cliffs, and stunning ocean vistas. Along the way, hikers can explore numerous hiking trails that offer breathtaking views of the park's forested valleys and coastal cliffs.

Another must-see natural wonder in Canada is Niagara Falls, which straddles the border between Canada and the

United States. Visitors can witness the awe-inspiring power of the falls from numerous vantage points, including a boat tour that takes them right up to the base of the falls.

Canada is also home to some of the world's largest and most beautiful lakes, including Lake Superior, which is the largest freshwater lake in the world by surface area. Other notable lakes include Lake Louise in Banff National Park, which is renowned for its vivid turquoise color, and Moraine Lake, which is surrounded by the majestic Canadian Rockies.

Cities and Towns Worth Visiting

In addition to its natural wonders, Canada is home to a number of vibrant and culturally rich cities and towns that are worth exploring. From the bustling metropolis of Toronto to the charming coastal town of Victoria, Canada's urban centers offer a diverse range of experiences for travelers.

Toronto, the largest city in Canada, is a vibrant hub of culture, art, and entertainment. Visitors can explore world-class museums, dine at renowned restaurants, and catch a show at the iconic Royal Ontario Museum. The city is also home to the famous CN Tower, which offers panoramic views of the city and surrounding Lake Ontario.

Montreal, Canada's second-largest city, is a cultural melting pot that blends French and English influences. Visitors can stroll through the historic Old Montreal district, explore the vibrant Plateau Mont-Royal neighborhood, or sample the city's renowned culinary scene.

Cultural and Historical Sites

Canada's rich history and diverse cultural heritage are reflected in its numerous cultural and historical sites. From ancient First Nations settlements to modern-day landmarks, Canada's cultural attractions au, Quebec, and is one of Canada's most visited museums.

The museum showcases the history, culture, and contributions of Canada's Indigenous peoples, as well as the country's French and English heritage. Visitors can explore the museum's exhibits, which include artifacts, interactive displays, and multimedia presentations that offer a fascinating look into Canada's past.

Another important cultural site in Canada is the Historic District of Old Québec, which is a UNESCO World Heritage Site. The district, which is located in Quebec City, is home to numerous historic buildings and landmarks, including the iconic Château Frontenac hotel and the Citadel, a 19th-century military fortress. Visitors can explore the narrow cobblestone streets and winding staircases of the district, which are lined with shops, restaurants, and galleries.

Canada is also home to numerous Indigenous cultural sites, including the Head-Smashed-In Buffalo Jump in Alberta. The site, which has been used by Indigenous peoples for thousands of years, features a cliff where bison were herded and then pushed over the edge, providing a vital source of food for the local communities. Visitors can explore the interpretive center and hiking trails that offer a glimpse into the rich history and culture of Canada's Indigenous peoples.

Overall, Canada's natural wonders, cities, and cultural attractions offer a diverse range of experiences for travelers. From hiking in the Canadian Rockies to exploring the vibrant neighborhoods of Toronto, there is something for everyone in this beautiful and fascinating country.

Permits, Fees, and Regulations

As with any outdoor activity, it is important to be aware of the permits, fees, and regulations associated with exploring Canada's national parks and other natural attractions.

National parks in Canada require visitors to purchase a park pass, which grants access to the park and its facilities. Passes can be purchased online, at park entrances, or at various retailers throughout the country. The cost of a park pass varies depending on the park and the length of the visit, but fees are typically based on a per-person or per-vehicle basis.

In addition to park passes, some national parks and other natural attractions in Canada require visitors to obtain permits for specific activities, such as camping or backcountry hiking. Permits may be required to ensure that the park or attraction can accommodate the number of visitors and to help protect the natural environment. It is important to check with the park or attraction before your visit to ensure that you have obtained all necessary permits.

Canada's national parks and other natural attractions also have various regulations in place to ensure the safety of visitors and the protection of the natural environment. For example, visitors may be required to follow certain rules related to camping, hiking, and wildlife viewing. It is important to familiarize yourself with these regulations before your visit to ensure that you are able to enjoy the park or attraction safely and responsibly.

In addition to regulations specific to individual parks and attractions, there are also general regulations that apply to outdoor activities throughout Canada. For example, visitors are required to follow Leave No Trace principles to minimize their impact on the natural environment. Visitors should also be aware of any fire bans or other restrictions related to outdoor fires, as these regulations can vary depending on the time of year and the location.

Overall, it is important to be aware of the permits, fees, and regulations associated with exploring Canada's natural wonders. By following these guidelines, visitors can help protect the natural environment and ensure a safe and enjoyable experience for themselves and others.

Dining Options

When it comes to dining options in Canada's national parks and other natural attractions, visitors have a variety of choices depending on their preferences and budget.

Many of Canada's national parks have on-site restaurants and cafes that offer a range of dining options, from casual fast food to fine dining. These restaurants often feature local and regional cuisine, showcasing the flavors and ingredients of the surrounding area. Some parks also have grocery stores or convenience stores where visitors can purchase snacks and other food items for their outdoor adventures.

For visitors who prefer to prepare their own meals, many of Canada's national parks also have campgrounds with cooking facilities, such as communal kitchens or fire pits. These facilities allow visitors to cook their own meals using their camping equipment or charcoal grills.

Outside of national parks, Canada's cities and towns offer a wide range of dining options, from international cuisine to local specialties. Some of Canada's most famous dishes include poutine, a hearty dish of french fries, gravy, and cheese curds; Nanaimo bars, a sweet dessert made with a chocolate and custard filling; and butter tarts, a pastry filled with a sweet mixture of butter, sugar, and eggs.

In addition to traditional dining options, Canada also has a vibrant food truck scene, with mobile kitchens serving up a variety of dishes in cities and towns across the country. Visitors can sample everything from gourmet burgers to sushi rolls from these food trucks, which often feature local and seasonal ingredients.

Overall, whether you're exploring Canada's national parks or its cities and towns, there are plenty of dining options to suit every taste and budget. From casual cafes to fine dining restaurants, visitors can enjoy the flavors and cuisine of this diverse and vibrant country.

Conclusion

Canada's National Parks are truly natural wonders that should not be missed by anyone who loves exploring the great outdoors. From the soaring peaks of the Rocky Mountains to the rugged coastlines of the Atlantic and Pacific, these parks offer some of the most breathtaking scenery and diverse wildlife in the world.

Whether you are an experienced hiker looking for a challenging trail or a family seeking a fun-filled adventure, Canada's National Parks have something for everyone. From the iconic Banff and Jasper National Parks to the lesser-known gems like Kootenay and Pacific Rim, each park offers its own unique beauty and opportunities for exploration.

Throughout this travel guide, we have highlighted some of the top attractions and must-see sights in each park, as well as provided practical tips and advice to help you make the most of your visit. We hope that this guide has inspired you to plan your own Canadian adventure and experience the wonder and beauty of these natural treasures for yourself.

So pack your bags, lace up your hiking boots, and get ready to explore the incredible natural wonders of Canada's National Parks. Whether you're seeking adventure, relaxation, or simply a chance to connect with nature, you won't be disappointed by the incredible experiences waiting for you in these magnificent parks.

TRAVEL PLANNERS

TRAVEL

DATE:
DURATION:

DESTINATION:

PLACES TO SEE:
1. _____
2. _____
3. _____
4. _____
5. _____
6. _____
7. _____

LOCAL FOOD TO TRY:
1. _____
2. _____
3. _____
4. _____
5. _____
6. _____
7. _____

DAY 1	DAY 2	DAY 3

DAY 4	DAY 5	DAY 6

NOTES

EXPENSES IN TOTAL:

PLANNER

TRAVEL

DATE:
DURATION:

DESTINATION:

PLACES TO SEE:	LOCAL FOOD TO TRY:
1 _____	1 _____
2 _____	2 _____
3 _____	3 _____
4 _____	4 _____
5 _____	5 _____
6 _____	6 _____
7 _____	7 _____

DAY 1	DAY 2	DAY 3

DAY 4	DAY 5	DAY 6

NOTES	EXPENSES IN TOTAL:

PLANNER

TRAVEL

DATE:
DURATION:

DESTINATION:

PLACES TO SEE:

1. _____
2. _____
3. _____
4. _____
5. _____
6. _____
7. _____

LOCAL FOOD TO TRY:

1. _____
2. _____
3. _____
4. _____
5. _____
6. _____
7. _____

DAY 1	DAY 2	DAY 3

DAY 4	DAY 5	DAY 6

NOTES

EXPENSES IN TOTAL:

PLANNER

TRAVEL

DATE:
DURATION:

DESTINATION:

PLACES TO SEE:	LOCAL FOOD TO TRY:
1	1
2	2
3	3
4	4
5	5
6	6
7	7

DAY 1	DAY 2	DAY 3

DAY 4	DAY 5	DAY 6

NOTES	EXPENSES IN TOTAL:

PLANNER

TRAVEL

DATE:
DURATION:

DESTINATION:

PLACES TO SEE:
1. _____
2. _____
3. _____
4. _____
5. _____
6. _____
7. _____

LOCAL FOOD TO TRY:
1. _____
2. _____
3. _____
4. _____
5. _____
6. _____
7. _____

DAY 1

DAY 2

DAY 3

DAY 4

DAY 5

DAY 6

NOTES

EXPENSES IN TOTAL:

PLANNER

TRAVEL

DATE:
DURATION:

DESTINATION:

PLACES TO SEE:
1. _____
2. _____
3. _____
4. _____
5. _____
6. _____
7. _____

LOCAL FOOD TO TRY:
1. _____
2. _____
3. _____
4. _____
5. _____
6. _____
7. _____

DAY 1

DAY 2

DAY 3

DAY 4

DAY 5

DAY 6

NOTES

EXPENSES IN TOTAL:

PLANNER

TRAVEL

DATE:
DURATION:

DESTINATION:

PLACES TO SEE:
1. _____
2. _____
3. _____
4. _____
5. _____
6. _____
7. _____

LOCAL FOOD TO TRY:
1. _____
2. _____
3. _____
4. _____
5. _____
6. _____
7. _____

DAY 1	DAY 2	DAY 3

DAY 4	DAY 5	DAY 6

NOTES

EXPENSES IN TOTAL:

PLANNER

TRAVEL

DATE:
DURATION:

DESTINATION:

PLACES TO SEE:	LOCAL FOOD TO TRY:
1 _____	1 _____
2 _____	2 _____
3 _____	3 _____
4 _____	4 _____
5 _____	5 _____
6 _____	6 _____
7 _____	7 _____

DAY 1	DAY 2	DAY 3

DAY 4	DAY 5	DAY 6

NOTES	EXPENSES IN TOTAL:

PLANNER

TRAVEL

DATE:
DURATION:

DESTINATION:

PLACES TO SEE:
1. _____
2. _____
3. _____
4. _____
5. _____
6. _____
7. _____

LOCAL FOOD TO TRY:
1. _____
2. _____
3. _____
4. _____
5. _____
6. _____
7. _____

DAY 1	DAY 2	DAY 3

DAY 4	DAY 5	DAY 6

NOTES

EXPENSES IN TOTAL:

PLANNER

TRAVEL

DATE:
DURATION:

DESTINATION:

PLACES TO SEE:
1. _____
2. _____
3. _____
4. _____
5. _____
6. _____
7. _____

LOCAL FOOD TO TRY:
1. _____
2. _____
3. _____
4. _____
5. _____
6. _____
7. _____

DAY 1	DAY 2	DAY 3

DAY 4	DAY 5	DAY 6

NOTES

EXPENSES IN TOTAL:

PLANNER

Printed in Great Britain
by Amazon